D0350627

# FENG SHUI

## for the classroom

# FENG SHUI
## for the classroom

by Debra Keller
Edited by Kelli F. Giammarco
Illustrated by Mary Ross

ARIEL BOOKS

**Andrews McMeel
Publishing**
Kansas City

# FENG SHUI
## for the classroom

## INTRODUCTION

Here's a test: Imagine you're an anxious new student stepping into your classroom for the first time. You hesitate outside the door, then cautiously walk in and look around. How does the room make you feel?

Are you instantly comforted and at ease? Do you feel confident, excited, motivated, inspired? What about connected, content, even lucky? If not, or if you're not sure, it's a good indication that your classroom could benefit from a healthy dose of Feng Shui.

Feng Shui is the ancient Chinese art of arranging an environment to affect positive changes in one's life. The words *Feng Shui* literally mean "wind and water"—two of the most important life-giving elements on earth. By applying the principles of Feng Shui to your classroom, you can create a life-giving atmosphere that can motivate, inspire, enrich, reward, support, comfort, and encourage both yourself and your students in untold ways.

Feng Shui is based on the belief that everything on earth is teeming with energy (called chi) and all energy seeks a state of balance. When active chi (yang) is in balance with passive chi (yin), harmony exists and life could not be better. Happiness abounds, relationships thrive, good health is abundant, and self-confidence (and school performance) soars.

Some people consider Feng Shui as an environmental science because it involves manipulating the physical elements of a space to create a positive psychological effect. Move furniture, add colors and objects, open pathways, circulate fresh air—when you mindfully alter the flow of energy in a room you can't help but affect how people feel within its walls. Done wisely, you can create a harmonious atmosphere that fosters all aspects of personal success.

In a classroom, Feng Shui can cause amazing things to happen. It may be as small as a reluctant child finally asking a question aloud, or as significant as a disinterested student awakening to the virtues of school. You may find yourself reading more inventive creative writing, or grading higher test scores, or enjoying more active listening, or seeing neater desks, or finding your room so quiet you could hear a pin drop—or simply feeling excited every day you go to work.

Although there are definite guidelines to Feng Shui, it's also an intuitive art. To begin you need only understand its basic principles, then trust yourself to apply them in whatever manner you feel best. Within this book you'll discover some age-old Feng Shui beliefs as well as modern classroom applications. Use them to jump-start your intuition and set your own ideas in motion.

Classroom Feng Shui is not difficult, and it doesn't require a huge time commitment. All it requires is common sense, compassion, awareness, and a desire to affect positive change—four qualities you, as a teacher, no doubt already have.

One of the simplest ways to begin applying the principles of Feng Shui is to determine your classroom's compass directions. Because each direction affects a different type of energy, Feng Shui experts recommend specific activities be conducted in specific areas of a room to achieve the most impact.

**Northwest:** When reading or lecturing you should typically stand (or sit) in the northwest area of your classroom facing southeast. This is the area of Wisdom and Knowledge and the traditional position of power and leadership.

**South:** If you have a student recognition wall in your classroom, make it the wall to the south. This is the Fame and Recognition area of your room and recognition here can be the most motivating.

**East:** The east wall of your classroom is the ideal place to hang children's artwork. East is the area of Children and Creativity—fill it artfully to inspire young imaginations.

**West:** The west side of your classroom is the area of Family and Health. Students with learning, health, or family problems should be seated here to help them gain the inner strength they need to overcome and succeed.

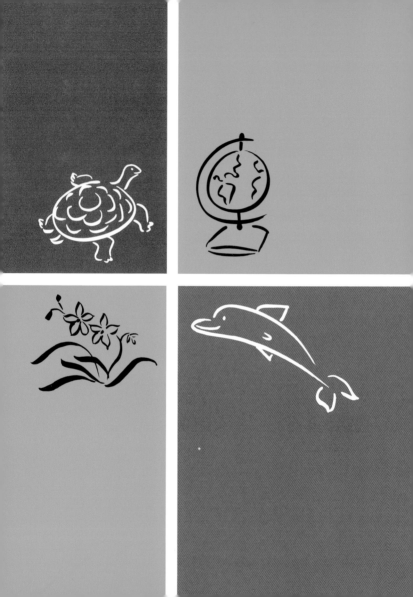

## THE LESSON OF LUCKY SEVEN

In Feng Shui, the number seven is associated with a thirst for learning. Keep seven symbols of wisdom in your classroom to enhance academic success. Here are seven to consider:

- Bamboo for inner strength
- A dragon for luck (most powerful in the east)
- A turtle for patience (best in the north)
- Dolphins for intelligence
- A globe for curiosity (best in the northeast)
- A phoenix for opportunity (most auspicious in the south)
- Orchids for bravery

## SEATS OF POWER

A teacher's desk should always face the classroom door. Not only will this allow you to keep a watchful eye out for tardiness, but the chi that flows between you and your class will encourage academic strength.

## NEVER TOO OLD FOR A FISH TANK

Even college students can benefit from the active chi of a fish tank, but be careful where you put it. Aquariums in the south or southeast encourage learning, but an aquarium to the right of a door can promote daydreams.

## THE CHI OF DESKS

The ideal desk is made of wood. Wood is filled with the energy of the earth and is accepting, supportive, and stable. Metal desks are mentally stimulating to a fault—they can exhaust mental energy if not tempered. Calm their chi by placing quartz crystals in the Earth areas of your classroom—the center, southeast, and northeast.

## THE POWER OF YELLOW

If you have a choice of what color to paint your classroom, you'd be wise to choose pale yellow. Yellow is the color of optimism, focus, and mental stimulation. In its paler shades it encourages active listening. Avoid yellows that are too sunshiny bright or you might wind up with way too much classroom chatter.

## CLUTTER VERSUS CHI

To understand the flow of classroom chi, think of the path of a river. Cluttered areas, or places laden with dust, act like boulders and beavers' dams—they block or slow the flow of chi so that energy downstream is reduced to a trickle. To maintain a healthy flow of chi, keep your classroom clean and clutter free.

## HIDDEN CLUTTER

Just because your classroom looks clutter free doesn't mean it is. Chi-draining clutter can lurk in the most unlikely places. Here are a few places to double check:

- Computer: How many files do you actually use?

- Pencil sharpener: When was the last time you emptied it?

- Tape: Do you have little bits and pieces stuck to your walls?

- Push pins: If they're not in use, remove them.

- Whiteboard: When you're done, wipe it clean.

## THE AREA OF WISDOM AND KNOWLEDGE

The most important area of your classroom to keep clutter free is the area of Wisdom and Knowledge—the northwest portion of your classroom. A healthy flow of chi here can motivate students, enrich self-confidence, and instill a lifelong love of learning. Dust and de-clutter it ASAP.

## BRIGHT BEGETS BRIGHT

Invigorate the chi in the northwest of your classroom with bright and shiny objects to ensure educational success. Consider a mirror, crystals, glass, silver, a desk lamp, or even a mylar balloon.

## THE EYES HAVE IT

The most auspicious arrangement for students' desks is in a semicircle facing you. Next best are offset rows (think of bricks in a wall). What's most important is that your students each have a clear view of you yet are able to interact with each other. Visual obstructions or communication barriers can block the flow of chi.

## THE VALUE OF BEING FLEXIBLE

Flexibility is not only key to effective teaching, it's also key to effective Feng Shui. Decorations and displays that are easily moved or changed keep students' interest high, classroom energy refreshed, and chi-gathering dust at bay.

## AU NATUREL

The more natural light in a classroom the better. Its chi is energizing and uplifting and can inspire students to reach new heights. If your windows are small (or worse, nonexistent), increase light levels with bright pictures, metal frames, mirrors, glass, and crystals. Refrain from turning on overhead lights unless you absolutely need them.

## GRAY MATTER

The most auspicious desk for an art, music, or creative writing teacher is one painted dove gray. According to the principles of Feng Shui, simple and serene dove gray supports creativity.

## PERSONAL SOUVENIRS

People learn best when they're light of spirit and open to the world around them. As a teacher, you set that tone. Keep something personal in your classroom to lighten your heart and brighten your smile. Your personal "souvenir" can be as small as a photo, postcard, or paperweight or as large as a special chair. But whatever it is, make sure it lifts your spirits enough to help you lighten those of your students.

## SENIORITY AND STANDING

The most auspicious place from which a teacher should teach (to lecture, read aloud, lead discussions) actually depends on your years on the job. Newer teachers should stand (or sit) in the east facing west. The chi energy of the east supports career growth and the realization of dreams. Experienced teachers should stand (or sit) in the northwest facing southeast. This is the classic Chinese position of leadership—the chi here enhances authority, builds trust and respect, and supports communication.

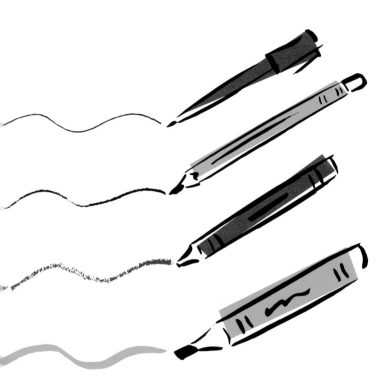

## POWER TOOLS

Tools of communication—pens, pencils, markers, crayons—are filled with water energy. They're strong, powerful, nurturing, and flexible. Keep plenty on hand to enhance your students' creativity and critical thinking skills.

## BACK SUPPORT

Always support your back to keep your spirit strong and enhance your inner strength. Place file cabinets and large cupboards behind your desk, hang a sweater or jacket from the back of your chair, or sit with your back to a supporting wall.

## BALANCING WOOD

Education is a wood activity. It's vital, active, cyclical work that inspires growth. But too much wood energy can cause you to take on too many projects, leaving you frustrated and exhausted. To balance the elements of a teacher's job, keep red or pointed fire symbols in the south: a pencil cup, a clay pot, stars, a pyramid.

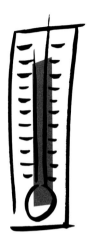

## A LESSON IN FAHRENHEIT

The Feng Shui of a room has as much to do with how it feels as how it looks. Regulate the temperature of your classroom daily according to the weather outside, but try to keep it slightly on the cool side. Cool air is decidedly yang and can help keep your students quick thinking and alert.

## ENHANCING COMPASSION

The most effective and memorable teachers are those who connect with their students. To enhance the relationships you have with your students, keep an appropriate Feng Shui symbol in the Compassion area of your desk—it's just to the right of your chair. Here are a few symbols to consider:

- A red pencil cup: Its fiery energy can fuel your empathy.

- A yellow box: Its earth energy can sharpen your listening skills.

- Silver scissors: Metal energy facilitates communication.

- A black tape dispenser: Use its water energy to heighten intuition.

- A green picture frame: Wood energy is the most nurturing of all.

## THE LESSON OF TWENTY-SEVEN

According to ancient Feng Shui beliefs, the number twenty-seven facilitates change. Before you begin any major classroom overhaul, move twenty-seven smaller items—paper, pencils, staplers, hole punchers—to help the relocation of the big stuff go smoothly.

## STOPPING DRAINS

If you have a sink in your classroom,
take care to close the drain or cover
it nightly. Open pipes are notorious
for draining healthy chi from a room.

## CLASSROOM HARMONY

Because education is active, classrooms are naturally more yang (active) than yin (quiet). Metal desks, uncomfortable chairs, hard floors, and computers all increase a room's yang energy. But as any teacher knows, too much activity can be exhausting! To help temper active energy and bring balance to your classroom, add a few yin touches: wicker baskets, a tapestry, rectangular pictures, or anything blue.

## FLOWER POWER

Flowers are a wonderful addition to any classroom, provided they're either fresh or silk. Dried flowers are overwhelmingly yin and can dampen students' enthusiasm to the point of putting some to sleep.

## CUTTING CHI

The sharp corners of bookshelves, counters, tables, and desks create cutting chi—imbalanced energy thrust outward like daggers. Avoid sharp edges if you can. If you can't, soften them with draping or rounded objects: vases, tablecloths, the drooping tendrils of plants. The less cutting chi you have in your classroom, the more supportive the learning environment.

### DE-PLASTICIZE

Plastic bins and trays may be common in modern classrooms but they have little place in Feng Shui. Plastics tend to block chi and stall the learning process. Instead store papers, workbooks, crayons—whatever—in wicker baskets. Baskets are a perfect blend of yin (weaving) and yang (wood) and can help students stay balanced and focused.

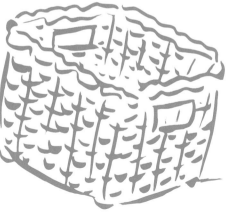

**THE POWER OF BLACK**

The most auspicious aquariums are those stocked with nine fish—eight that are orange, silver, striped, or bright colors and one that is black to absorb negative chi.

## RESOLVE

To give your students a healthy dose of ambition, keep tall plants in the northeast part of your classroom. This is the area of New Beginnings and tall plants here encourage resolve.

## FOUR SEASONS OF FENG SHUI

At the heart of Feng Shui is the basic notion that energy is in a continual state of change and to reap the most from it you need to change along with it. To this end, keep at least one Feng Shui symbol in your classroom that changes with the seasons. Here are a few suggestions:

**Autumn:** Something round and white in the west can help focus energy inward and prepare students for a year of discovery. Try a polished stone, a pale-colored globe, or white marbles in a shallow bowl.

**Winter:** Something curvy and dark blue or black in the north can help energy grow within and give students a sense of well-being. Try ocean-themed artwork, graceful black bookends, or a roll of blue corrugated cardboard.

**Spring:** Something green and rectangular in the east or southeast can help direct energy outward, bolstering students' confidence in time for exams. Try a tall leafy plant (bamboo is especially auspicious), a lean vase or pitcher, or a green pedestal.

**Summer:** Something red and triangular in the south makes energy flow upward, helping students acquire a lot of knowledge in a short period of time. Try a pyramid-shaped paperweight, a bell with a handle, or a small lamp with a conical red shade.

## EIGHT DIRECTIONS

The most auspicious shaped room is an octagon—in Feng Shui terms, its eight walls create a perfect balance that fosters luck and success. To turn a four-sided classroom into an auspicious octagon place a mirror in each of the four corners.

## HOW DOES YOUR INDOOR GARDEN GROW?

Indoor plants are a wonderful way to keep classroom energy vital and boredom at bay, but be mindful of their growth habit. If you prefer trailing plants, like spider plants and ivy, keep them neatly trimmed and out of the custodian's way.

## NEVER PUT A DESK . . .

- Under a shelf
- Under a heat or air-conditioning vent
- Under a beam

## THE APPLE OF YOUR EYE

An apple on your desk might be a Western cliché, but in terms of classroom Feng Shui, it makes sense. Apples are round, red, hard, and shiny—all of which are yang qualities. Keeping an apple (edible or not) on your desk can help keep your concentration sharp and your eye for details keen so you're quick, alert, and ready to roll with the mood of the day no matter what mood your students may be in.

## GEOLOGY 101

Every classroom rock collection should include at least one quartz crystal. Quartz crystals are one of the most powerful activators of stagnant chi. Even uncut, they refract the colors of the rainbow and reflect chi in all directions. Cut crystals are especially useful when hung in a corner—they enliven students and encourage creativity.

## THE CHI OF COLORS

When making name tags for your students' desks or cubbies, be mindful of the colors you choose and the energies they effect. Here are some simple Feng Shui guidelines:

- Red enhances friendliness. It's ideal for a shy person or group.

- Yellow promotes warmth. A good color to begin the year with or to soften the rough edges of a bully.

- Green increases activity. Use it wisely and sparingly.

- Blue fosters communication. A marvelous choice for a multicultural (or multiage or multiability) class.

- Purple enhances success. A terrific color overall but especially in creative environments.

## SNACK-TIME CHI

Teachers of young children can affect the energy of their class by serving snacks that either reinforce or counteract the prevailing mood of the day. Salty yang snacks (pretzels, peanut butter, many kinds of cheese) promote activity while sweet yin snacks (fruit, cookies, cereal, juice) can induce quiet and calm.

## RECYCLE

Full or overflowing recycle bins harbor a wealth of stagnant chi. Empty them often (even midday if you have to) to keep your students interested and alert.

## SECURITY

To help boost your students' self-esteem and allow them to express themselves freely, keep charcoal (think drawing pencils, not barbecue briquettes) in the southeast part of your classroom. This is the area of Communication and charcoal here boosts security.

## THE POWER OF PLANTS

It's important to purify the air in a classroom to keep energy fresh and impurities at bay. Open the windows daily if you can, and consider growing a houseplant or two. Here are a few to consider:

- Peace lily: Filled with metal energy, it neutralizes radiation from computers.

- Heart leaf philodendron: Its soil energy helps create a stable atmosphere.

- Boston fern: Its fiery energy acts like a fan in helping circulate healthy chi.

- English ivy: Like a breath of fresh air, its water energy calms and relaxes.

- Ficus: Its tree absorbs toxins and infuses the air with life-giving oxygen.

## THE CHI OF BOOKS

Painful as it may be, parting with old books is one of the best things you can do to keep classroom chi healthy and vibrant. Old, unread, or outdated books can wreak havoc in school—they collect dust, add to clutter, and can depress the whole learning process. But take heart—if you cull through your bookshelf once a year and donate the books you no longer use, you'll give someone else a chance to love those books too.

## SHEDDING LIGHT ON LEARNING

Fluorescent lighting is commonplace in classrooms but, ironically, is the worst type, according to Feng Shui. Of all artificial lighting, it emits the most radiation, which can completely drain mental energy. To help offset its negative effects, keep a full-spectrum light in the front of your classroom within view of all your students.

## CLASSROOM PETS

Teachers of young children should choose classroom pets wisely. Pets in general have a huge effect on the energy of a room, and different animals affect chi in different ways.

- Goldfish are very auspicious and are said to attract success.

- Turtles and tortoises promote patience.

- Birds attract happiness and foster friendships.

- Bunnies promote communication and self-assurance.

- Frogs attract wealth.

- Reptiles heighten intuition.

- Guinea pigs and hamsters foster wisdom.

- Mice and rats deepen intellectual understanding.

## SEA SALT

Although incense and scented candles are popular tools for infusing the air with positive chi, it's best to avoid them in a classroom. You never know what your students' allergies may be. Instead, keep a small clay bowl filled with sea salt on your desk to absorb negative chi and purify the air.

## HARMONY

To help you grow healthy relationships with your students, keep a ticking clock in the southwest part of your classroom. This is the area of Relationships and clocks here encourage harmony.

## TRANQUILLITY

To help your students handle stress and find a means of reducing anxiety, keep white flowers in the north part of your classroom. This is the area of Inner Journeys and white flowers here promote tranquillity.

## FIX IT

Broken things are magnets for negative chi. Make a weekly check of your classroom to keep things in working order. Does your projector work? What about that slow-rolling computer mouse? And when you pull down the map does it roll right back up? The few minutes you spend fixing things can result in days of academic harmony.

## THE POWER OF COLOR

Use color to influence the energy of your classroom according to your lesson plan. Writing, taking notes, and exams are yang activities and are more easily achieved with warm and bright objects nearby (a red flag, a bowl of oranges, a yellow ribbon). Reading and discussing are more yin and are enhanced by cool colors and pastels (green leaves, a blue vase, purple flowers, a pink bowl). In Feng Shui, color is enormously powerful—the smallest touch can have a huge effect on the psychology of everyone in a room.

## OPEN MINDS

Refrain from hanging your students' artwork in windows unless the artwork lets in natural light (like tissue-paper collages). If wall space is at a minimum and you feel you absolutely must use windows to display things, position the artwork in the lower portion so students can still see the sky. Open views foster open minds.

## THE CHI OF SPACE

Don't feel compelled to fill every square inch of wall space with a display. Chi requires open space in order to flow freely. Remember, in Feng Shui, less is often a whole lot more.

## SHADOWS AND CHI

If your classroom lies in the shadow of a neighboring building, the darkness that falls can affect the chi within. Fortunately, there are remedies you can use to correct the situation.

- If the shadow is cast from the east, it may diminish your room's tree energy and leave your students feeling insecure. Water features, baskets, and bright green objects can restore their academic confidence.

- If the shadow is cast from the south, it can deplete your room of fire energy and cause students to feel apathetic. Tall plants, wooden objects, and the color purple can restore their passion for learning.

- If the shadow is cast from the west, it can rob your room of metal energy and leave your students disorganized and discontent. Granite, metals, and the color white can improve their mood and habits.

## STEMMING THE FLOW

If you have more than one classroom
door, place something between them
(a table, a chair, a bookcase) to stop
fresh chi from streaming in one door
and flowing right out the other.

## THE MAGIC OF MIRRORS

If your classroom has large windows but they all face north your students may not be getting the light they need to perform at their best. Hang mirrors to help lighten your room and circulate chi, but be careful where you put them. In Feng Shui, reflections signify abundance—make sure your mirrors don't reflect your students or you may end up feeling drained and overwhelmed.

## WIND CHIMES

Even indoors, wind chimes can be a powerful chi activator. Their sound waves stir the air and circulate chi, and their tone purifies and cleanses. Choose classroom chimes carefully—their sound should be clear, sweet, and light to inspire students to do their best.

## WATER

Water is one of the most potent of all Feng Shui tools. A classroom water feature brings in fresh chi that can improve your students' health, enhance their natural talents, and positively affect their destiny. Consider a fishbowl, a tabletop fountain, or even a small bowl of water on a windowsill (just remember to refill it daily).

## A BREATH OF FRESH AIR

When you step into your classroom each morning, throw open whatever doors and windows you can and take a breath of fresh air. Not only will it ready you for the challenges of your day, but it will fill your classroom with the fresh, vital energy your students need to succeed.

## THE WAY NATURE INTENDED

The more natural the materials in your classroom, the more conducive to learning it is. Cover linoleum counters with woven mats, toss a rug or two on a linoleum floor. If you're a preschool or early elementary teacher, keep plenty of soft, natural fiber pillows around for your young students to sink into or cuddle. But be sure to keep natural fabrics clean and dust free to ensure your classroom chi is healthy and alive.

## A LITTLE GOES A LONG WAY

Classrooms should generally be lighter, brighter, noisier, and more alive than a quiet place of study, like a library. This means they should lean toward the yang. Use a light hand when harmonizing your classroom's energy with yin objects—a few yin touches go a long way.

## PERSONAL SPACE

It's not just your classroom you need to be mindful of when applying the principles of Feng Shui. Remember to keep yourself in the equation as well! Create a pleasing personal space for yourself. You are, after all, the key to all success and it's vital you feel your best each day too.

THIS BOOK WAS DESIGNED
AND TYPESET IN UNIVERS
BY ANN ZIPKIN OF ANN-DESIGN,
KATONAH, NEW YORK.